Space Between My Teeth

Space Between My Teeth

✦

Funny Poems for Kids

J. Ellen Fedder

iUniverse, Inc.
New York Lincoln Shanghai

Space Between My Teeth
Funny Poems for Kids

Copyright © 2005 by J. Ellen Fedder

iUniverse books may be ordered through booksellers or by contacting:

iUniverse
2021 Pine Lake Road, Suite 100
Lincoln, NE 68512
www.iuniverse.com
1-800-Authors (1-800-288-4677)

ISBN: 0-595-34476-3

Printed in the United States of America

Dedicated in loving memory
to my father, whose humor touched my heart
and to my mother, whose heart touched my humor.

Contents

Eat It Up

Space between My Teeth

I have a space between my teeth
That lets the milkshake in,
And I don't even need a straw
Or napkin for my chin.

It's great for whistles and it is
My pencil holding spot.
It saves on toothpaste cuz' I can't
Brush what I haven't got.

Can't Control Me

Like a coin purse full of pennies
I have eaten far too much.
For it seems I can't control me,
I eat everything I touch.

Like a sock tub full of stockings,
I am never empty long.
For it seems I can't control me,
I eat everything all wrong.

Like a freebie in the mail,
I just gotta' try it out.
For it seems I can't control me,
Food is what my life's about.

Picky Eater

My sister never cleans her plate
Unless it's pizza night.
She is a picky eater and
Our food is seldom right.

She never eats the foreign stuff
Or mixed up casseroles.
She never touches pickled food
Or anything with holes.

It's really not a problem when
She won't eat this or that.
I'm really quick to offer help.
That's how I got so fat.

Vegetarian

I am a vegetarian.
I like my food from plants.
But just the other evening,
I ate celery with ants.

I ate my salad bowl of greens,
Then munched my apple through,
Before I noticed half the worm
That I had bit in two.

So now I wonder if I am
A vegetarian,
Since I have eaten food that crawls,
And maybe might again.

Breakfast Share

On Saturday for breakfast we
Have bacon, toast, and eggs
And sit around the table while
Our fleabag woofs and begs.

I slip him bits of bacon,
And my sister gives him fat.
She always keeps the meaty ones,
And feeds them to her cat.

My mother never gets to sit.
She's in the kitchen cuz'
We like our eggs all different and
They're not the way she does.

It's over easy for my dad,
And mine stay in the shell.
My brother and my sister like
Them scrambled really well.

The baby's eggs are bite size and
My mom's are poached a bit.
The dog sits by the high chair and
He gets his share of it.

Biscuit Experiment

My sister made me biscuits.
They were hard and they were big,
Cuz' she tried a new experiment
And I'm her guinea pig.

I couldn't even bite one,
And it wouldn't even suck.
But it really came in handy
For my practice hockey puck.

Baking Mess

My sister always makes a mess
From head to toe and more.
Whenever she's allowed to bake,
There's flour on the floor,

And on her nose and in her hair,
And egg shells in the sink,
And chocolate on the windowsill
And oven door, I think.

And all the pots and mixing bowls
Get dirty when she bakes,
Which isn't very often with
The clean up that it takes.

Life's Little Annoyances

When I Lost

My mom says I'm forgetful cuz'
I lose things every day,
Like when I lost my sister from
The backyard where we play,

And when I lost my swimsuit in
The city swimming pool,
And when I lost my puppy on
The shortcut to my school,

And when I lost the car keys down
The bathroom toilet drain,
And when I lost my lizard by
The lady on the plane.

My mama says I'd lose my head,
Except it's fastened on.
Without my brain, how would I find
My head if it was gone?

Awful Noise

I hear an awful noise.
It sounds just like a crow,
Or maybe it's a cow.
I'm sure that I don't know.

"Say, Mom, what is that noise?
Is something dying fast?"
"It's just your brother dear,
And that's a trombone blast."

Little Chore

I have a little chore.
It's really quite a bore.
It stinks and nothing more.
I do it cuz' I'm poor.

With bucket and a scoop,
And eyeballs of a snoop,
The backyard's where I troop,
To shovel up the poop!

A Bit Behind

When Mom tells me to clean the house,
We end up losing stuff.
Then I must play detective and
The clues are pretty tough,

Cuz' I don't even plan to lose
The stuff I gotta' find.
It happens when I'm running just
A little bit behind,

Like when I put toothpaste in
The frigerator door
And when I put the milk jug in
The closet on the floor.

To find the stuff that's missing
I must go back to the crime,
Retrace my steps from somewhere,
And I find it all the time.

Half a Room

I share a bedroom and a bath
And boy it's really tough,
Cuz' my half doesn't equal half
And his has all the stuff.

The tapeline down the middle shows
The line I dare not cross.
And since he's got a year on me,
He says that he's the boss.

I get to use the window and
He gets to use the door.
His clothes hang in the closet and
My clothes hang on the floor.

I get to use the shower stall.
He gets the bathroom sink.
But using half the toilet seat
Is really dumb I think.

Just a Minute

Just a minute, means an hour,
When my sister's in the shower.
And it means a whole lot more,
When I'm pounding on the door.

Be right out, means not a chance,
Cuz' she loves to make me dance.
And it means, I'll be a while,
So just cross your legs and smile.

That's Enough

Where is the hand remote?
It can't just walk away.
I'd better have it quick,
Or someone's gonna' pay!

I need a good cartoon.
This program's got no kick.
I've gotta' change it soon,
Or else I will be sick.

My dad says, "That's enough!
Why don't you try some sweat?
Just get up off your duff,
And change it at the set!"

I Hate List

I made a list the other day
Of things I hate to do.
I think they are a waste of time.
You probably do, too.

I really hate to make my bed.
I hate to comb my hair.
I hate to hang up clothing and
To change my underwear.

My list is not complete cuz' I
Remembered as I wrote,
The thing I hate to do the most
Is write down any note.

Slow Children

The road crew came by yesterday
And placed a yellow sign.
Of all the houses on this block,
Why right in front of mine?

It says "SLOW CHILDREN" plain and clear
And I don't think it's cool,
Cuz' I'm not slow, I got an A
In penmanship at school.

Pets and Pals

Tasty Snacks

I have a pet I like to train
With treats and tasty snacks.
My pet can do a lot of tricks
Like one foot jumping jacks.

He's never very bashful when
The neighbors come to see.
If they just bring the tasty snacks
The pet I train is me.

Mystery Friend

My little sister's got a friend
That I have never met.
She comes and goes most every day
Though I've not seen her yet.

According to my sister, we
Should really let her stay,
Cuz' she is very helpful and
She'd not be in the way.

I hid behind the curtain just
To solve the mystery,
But never saw a single thing,
When I peeked out to see.

My sister's got a see-through friend.
No problem, I don't care.
But see-through friend had better move.
She's sitting in my chair.

Dog Bed

The dog is on the bed,
He's moving toward my head.
Just how am I to catch my zzz's
With fleabag, if you please?

The dog now licks my face.
He aims to take my place.
He does his spin and settles in,
Where my head should have been.

Jerky Toys

My dog barks at total strangers
And most anything on legs,
Like the squirrels and the neighbors,
As he wags his tail and begs.

Seems he can't decide who's friendly
And who needs to stay away.
So he barks and wags his tail,
When he'd really like to play.

Neighbors say they'd like some quiet,
Even though he's really sweet.
Trouble is he won't come to me,
Not without a doggie treat.

Now he's got it figured out.
Hungry, means go make some noise,
Cuz' he knows that I'll reward him
With his favorite jerky toys.

Kitten Lump

Have you seen my little kitten?
I have looked both high and low.
I have asked my older brother,
And he says he doesn't know.

Come here kitty, kitty, kitty
Little kitty where are you?
Are you hiding in the bathtub?
Are you sleeping in my shoe?

Now I know you're very clever.
So I have to think this through,
Think about the funny places
That a kitten might get to.

All this thinking makes me sleepy.
I have gotta' get some rest.
Hey! My pillow is all lumpy!
Guess my kitten likes it best.

Cat Fur

My little cat has milk-white fur.
It's very plain to see,
For on my new black outfit
I have white accessory.

Sheep Riddle

If Mary had a little lamb
And Bo Peep lost her sheep,
Then could it be that Mary's lamb
Was not her sheep to keep?

Jumping Trick

There's a doggie at the window
Just-a-begging to come in.
She's-a-wagging and a smiling,
With her brown-eyed doggie grin.

She's so cute; you gotta' love her,
Even with her dirty paws.
And I never really mind it when
She snags things with her claws.

But my mother does, believe me.
So I'll try to clean up quick,
Once I play a little with her and
Reward her jumping trick.

Watch the vase! Oh not the table!
That was dinner for my Dad.
Bet you're glad that you don't live here,
Cuz' my mom will be sooo mad!

Stuck Here

There's a spider in my closet
And a spider on the door.
There's another on my curtain
And a big one on the floor.

So I'm stuck here in my bedroom
Sitting safely on my bed,
Cuz' I'm sure if I move any,
I'll have spiders on my head.

Now I wonder why they don't move,
And why they won't spin a web?
Maybe they are busy sleeping,
Or perhaps they're just plain dead?

Well, I think that I will chance it.
Here I go. Where will I land?
Out the door and there's my brother,
Plastic spiders in his hand.

Looking Good

New Pants

I like to slide down banisters
And climb the tallest trees.
I like to glide on icy streets
And crawl upon my knees.

But Mama says I gotta' make
These pants last for a while,
Since every other pair I've got
Is in the mending pile.

So how's a kid to be a kid
Unless he gets to crawl,
And slide and climb and jump and glide?
I like to do them all.

I'll take a chance with my new pants
And still go out to play,
Cuz' I don't care about the holes.
I like my pants that way.

Frazzled

My sister got a permanent.
I'm trying to be kind.
She looks a little frazzled and
I'm not exactly blind.

The laugh I'm holding in is more
Than I can barely take.
I've gotta' leave the room or else
I'm gonna' nearly shake.

The baseball cap up on the shelf
Right by the laundry door,
I planned to wear myself but now,
I think she needs it more.

Best Word

Daddy's from the East Coast.
Mama's from the West.
I'm the one who really knows
The word that says it best.

Daddy says a sofa,
Mama says love seat.
I say couch potato as
I'm propping up my feet.

Daddy drinks a soda.
Mama sips a pop.
I gulp root beer from the can
And guzzle every drop.

Daddy draws the water.
Mama fills the tub.
I just take a shower and I
Never even scrub!

Aches and Pains

These Allergies

Rashes make me scratch.
Sneezes make me twitch.
Since I got these allergies,
Seems all I do is itch.

Sneezing until noon,
Itching constantly,
I don't have these allergies.
These allergies have me.

Bottom Blue

My swing set broke the other day
And I was on it, too.
I found the ground was rocky and
It turned my bottom blue.

A bruise upon the rumpus is
A bruise no one can see.
So no one really knows how sore
I really am, but me.

Sleepless

I've found the perfect answer for
The nights I cannot sleep.
It's not a glass of lukewarm milk.
It's not me counting sheep.

I simply grab my flashlight
And I read things in the night,
Like comic books and funnies,
After mom turns out the light.

Middle Ache

In the middle of the night,
In the middle of the hour,
My middle took a pain and I
Felt a little sour.

I tried to just ignore it,
But it wouldn't go away.
So I sat up in my bed and
Decided then to pray.

Oh Lord, I need your help,
For I think I'm gonna' die,
If I don't get to the kitchen,
For that final piece of pie.

Kid Proof

My grandma has me open all
The bottles on her shelf,
So I can get the kid-proof pills
She cannot get herself.

And she has trouble reading all
The labels on the back.
So that is why she asks for me,
Cuz' I've just got the knack.

Catch a Cold

How do you catch a cold?
I need to know the trick.
For I have never seen a cold
And I must catch one quick.

I need a cold today.
Tomorrow is a test.
So help me please, catch a disease.
The one-day kind is best.

Fire Expert

I am a fire expert all
The firemen agree.
They say I've been to hard knock school
And earned my first degree.

I know the things that make a blaze
And things that just make smoke.
And I can tell you every one that
Makes a family choke.

You never push the chubby bread
Down in the toaster slot.
You never put a shirt on high
And microwave it hot.

You never dry your mittens in
The oven when they're damp.
You never make it darker with
A blanket on the lamp.

My mama says she hopes that all
My training stuff is done,
Cuz' she would like to please avoid
The calls to 9–1–1.

Night-Light

My sister's got a night-light just
In case she's gotta' go,
In the middle of the night so she
Won't trip or stub her toe.

I know the real reason for
The night-light on her wall.
It's monsters in her closet and
It's tigers down the hall.

I never need a night-light cuz'
I check my room before
I turn the light out for the night
And close my bedroom door.

House Rules

Parents Say

Money doesn't grow on trees!
Got no stock in companies!
Use your brain! You've got to think!
Take a bath! You really stink!

Eat us out of house and home!
Time is up! Get off the phone!
Children starving, clean your plate!
Hurry up or you'll be late!

Help your brother! Do your share!
No one says that life is fair!
Never finish 'til you start!
Seems I know these all by heart.

Pig Award

My brother wins the pig award.
His bedroom is a mess.
Don't ask the color of his rug,
Cuz' I would hafta' guess.

I haven't seen his clothing clean
In quite a little while,
Cuz' he can't seem to get it to
The weekly laundry pile.

And now we're running short of forks
And plates to have a meal.
I bet they're underneath his bed.
Will you reach in and feel?

Stuck Here

Seems I've got a little problem
With my bedroom storage space.
I've filled every single cubby.
I've used every single place.

I've got posters over posters.
I've got hangers hung on clothes.
I've got sheets on top of blankets.
It just multiplies and grows.

Well, my parents say I'm stuck here
'Til they see the bedroom floor.
And they brought these plastic trash bags,
Saying there are plenty more.

So I sit here in the middle
Of this masterpiece and moan,
For I cannot see a single thing
I'd trash, or sell, or loan.

Short Stack

My Mama says my stack is short
With only three or four.

My stack should be much taller.
It should stack up several more.

A week has seven days and so
My stack ought to have too,

Seven pair of underwear or
Else I have too few.

I'm Confused

My mother's always early and
My father's always late.
The dog is always ready and
The baby makes us wait.

My mother says its social to
Be early, just a bit.
But father says it never starts
Until he gets to it.

Now I'm confused about the time
And whether to be late,
Or early, or be ready quick,
Or just make people wait.

Money Matters

Car Trip Contest

Now my Mama has a contest
That she thinks is really cool,
And she says that I can win it
On this car trip to my school.

Not one word or little giggle,
Not a cough or funny sneeze,
Can I make to win the contest.
Now this prize should be a breeze.

When I win, I get a movie
I can rent this afternoon.
One more mile and it is mine!
It had better happen soon,

For my mouth is full of noise.
All the words are coming fast.
I am never going to make it.
I am never going to last.

Oh, hey, mom, I got a question.
Can we try it for one block?
I am not a quiet person,
And my mouth just wants to talk.

Fire in My Pocket

I have a little money
That I earned just yesterday,
And I'd really like to spend it
But the store's so far away.

There's a yard sale going on
At the neighbor's house next door.
Do you think there might be something
That I could be looking for?

Get a load of all this stuff!
It's enough to make me shout.
There's a fire in my pocket
And I gotta' let it out!

Cut a Deal

My chores include the dishes for
Our Friday evening meal,
The rinsing and the stacking too,
Unless I cut a deal.

My sister is a saver so
I sometimes got it made.
She'll do the dishes for me just
As long as she gets paid.

She likes her bills in big ones so
I hafta' plan ahead,
Or sweeten up the deal some
By making up her bed.

Empty Spot

When shopping with my dad,
I get the same reply.
Seems every time I ask for stuff,
He tells me no, and why.

The budget says I'm broke.
There is no money tree.
My wallet has an empty spot,
And there's no change on me.

But what about a check?
I asked the other day.
I see you've got a lot of those,
That you could use to pay.

Mail Winner

My name is on this letter that
The postman brought today.
It says I've won a million bucks!
Now I can *really* play.

Just think of all the cool machines,
The gadgets and the toys.
Imagine all the techno stuff
At stores for girls and boys.

I wonder when they'll send it,
All that money meant for me,
Cuz' I really want to spend it.
Do you think there'll be a fee?

Let me read the little print.
It says, to win you've gotta' pay.
Just a million and a half
Buys you another chance to play.

Family for Sale

Ya' wanna' buy a family?
I've got one really cheap.
My sister is a knucklehead.
My brother is a creep.

No wait, I really mean to say,
My sister is a steal,
And if you take the both of them,
I'll give you quite a deal.

My parents cost a little more,
And baby is for free.
But wait, I guess, if you take them,
You might as well take me.

Passing Time

Gone Fishing

Grandpa is a funny guy.
I like to watch him fish.
I think he bought the tackle shop,
Or maybe that's his wish.

Grandpa's got a lot of bait
Of every kind and breed.
I think he's got most everything
A fisherman might need.

Grandpa tells me stories
Of the ones that got away.
Seems the only thing he's catching
Is an awful cold today.

The Thing

Every scrap of paper,
Every piece of string,
Every toilet paper tube is
Stuff to make the "THING."

Duct tape helps a little.
Glitter helps a lot.
I'm not certain what it is, but
I know what it's not.

Camping Out Back

The smell of the woods,
The feel of the breeze,
Camping is great,
Out under the trees.

Pitching a tent,
Stowing my gear,
Rolling a bag,
Nothing to fear,

Fishing the pond,
Franks on the grill,
Eating outdoors,
Can't get my fill.

Flashlight I see,
Mom with a snack,
Too bad I'm just
Camping out back.

Pocket Stuff

They never make my pockets big
Enough for all the things
I find outside in nature, like
This rock with all these rings.

And here's a rock, I think is gold,
And here's a dead fish gill,
Two feathers, and a snail shell
For on my windowsill.

If only I had pockets that
Could hold a little more
I'd never need to stuff my socks
Outside the front step door.

Wall Questions

A kid can spend a lot of time
Just staring at the wall
And thinking up the questions and
The answers to them all.

I sometimes ask my dad about
A question that I've had,
And he says I should ask my mom,
And she says ask my dad.

And if I ask my sister, it
Will cost me fifty cents.
And I can't ask my brother cuz'
My brother's kinda' dense.

And if I ask the baby, I
Get smiles and a coo.
But doggie knows the answer,
For a little doggie chew.

Blanket Fort

I like to make a fort out of
The cushions from the chair,
And cushions from the couch and all
The blankets we can spare.

I make it in the middle of the
Living room and then
I crawl inside with flashlights and
A notebook and a pen.

And just in case I need a snack,
I grab a few of those.
And last of all I get the dog,
Cuz' where I am, he goes.

The last time that I made a fort
I plum forgot the dog,
And had a "ceiling visitor"
When he played leaping frog.

Entertain Myself

I'm never very bored for long.
There's lots of stuff to do
To entertain myself a bit
With something fresh and new.

For instance, if I take the fan
And push the button, "FAST"
And talk into the front of it,
I really have a blast.

And if I nibble crackers and
I keep the crumbs all dry
Inside my mouth and then I blow,
The shower crumbs all fly.

And if I pick the puffs
From all the dandelion weeds,
And make a big bouquet and blow,
It rains down little seeds.

But one thing I have learned about
A dandelion puff,
I never face the wind or I
Am covered with the stuff.

Party Crash

A slumber party is a blast.
I love them, every one.
But I am not invited; I
Just crash them all for fun.

Especially when my sister is
The hostess for the night.
It's guaranteed to make her mad
And start a pillow fight.

My favorite thing to do at one
Is set my pet snake free.
You ought to hear the screaming when
My snake crawls up a knee.

Funny Beast

I see a large rhinoceros
With rhinestone earrings on.
It's really not preposterous.
I'm lying on my lawn,

Just watching clouds float overhead
A mile in the sky.
It's gotta' be my favorite thing
To help the hours go by.

I see another funny beast,
Unusual and hard,
A pink flamingo on one leg,
Right in my neighbor's yard!

0-595-34476-3

CPSIA information can be obtained at www.ICGtesting.com
Printed in the USA
LVOW092137050312

271748LV00003B/135/A